P9-BUI-840

The Keto Instant Pot Cookbook

Easy Keto Diet Instant Pot Recipes with Only 6 Ingredients or Less to Help You Lose Weight Quickly

By

Carolyn Stewart

Copyrights ©2018 by Carolyn Stewart

All rights reserved.

No part of this guide may be reproduced in any form without permission in writing from the publisher except in the case of brief quotations embodied in critical articles or reviews.

Legal & Disclaimer

The information and contents herein are not designed to replace or take the place of any form of medical or professional advice and are not meant to replace the need for independent medical, financial, legal or other professional advice or services, as may be required. The content and information in this book have been provided for educational and entertainment purposes only.

The content and information in this book have been compiled from reliable sources and are accurate to the author's best knowledge, information, and belief. The author cannot guarantee this book's accuracy and validity and cannot be held liable for any errors and/or omissions. Further, changes will be periodically made to this book when needed. It is recommended that you consult with a health professional who is familiar with your personal medical history before using any of the suggested remedies, techniques, or information in this book.

Upon using the contents in this book, you agree to hold harmless the author from and against any damages, costs, and expenses, including any legal fees potentially resulting from the application of the information provided You agree to accept all risks associated with using the information presented inside this book.

Table of Contents

Introduction

The ketogenic diet has become one of the most popular diets out there, and for good reason. The simple fact of the matter is that it works!

If you're not familiar with the diet, the most important thing you need to know is that it is a natural (and effective) way to encourage your body to burn your stored fat. Basically, you change your eating habits to reduce your carbohydrate intake and increase your fat intake. This switch forces your body to change over from burning glucose for fuel to burning through your stored fat.

Let's take a closer look at how this process works.

When you eat food, your body immediately starts breaking it down into smaller components that can be digested and absorbed. Carbohydrates are made up of glucose molecules which are quickly absorbed into the bloodstream. When your blood sugar levels rise, it triggers your pancreas to produce a hormone called insulin which helps your cells absorb glucose from your blood to use it as energy.

As your cells absorb the glucose, your blood sugar levels taper back down to their normal level, and your insulin levels go down as well.

Unfortunately, the staples of the typical Western diet (high-carb foods) result in chronically elevated blood sugar levels which leads to a number of problems, including obesity. That's where the ketogenic diet comes in.

When you reduce your carb intake, you're forcing your body to find an alternative source of fuel. In the case of the ketogenic diet, a high-fat diet, your body will convert to burning fat for fuel – including your stored fat. You don't even have to count calories or do a lot of exercise. All you really need to do is make sure that you're consuming between 70% and 80% fat, up to 20% protein, and no more than 5% carbohydrates.

The ketogenic diet is great for fat burning, but that's not all it does. Here is a quick summary of some of the other benefits:

- Improved cardiovascular health markers like blood pressure and cholesterol.
- Protection for the brain against neurodegenerative diseases.
- Reduced risk for certain types of cancer.
- Improved microflora in the digestive tract for more regular digestion.
- Regulated blood sugar and insulin levels, fewer diabetic complications.
- Better mood and relief from psychological disorders like anxiety.
- Improved concentration and focus, lower stress levels.

The ketogenic diet is extremely effective and, while it may take some getting used it, you'll love it in no time at all.

If you're just starting out on the keto diet, there are some things you'll need to do to encourage your body to enter a state of ketosis – that's when it will be optimized for burning fat. Here are some tips to get started with keto:

- Slowly reduce your carbohydrate intake, so you don't shock your system – start by making one meal a day keto and work your way up.
- As you decrease your carbohydrate intake, start eating more fat – focus on healthy fats from avocado, olive oil, and MCT oil.
- Take a 15 to 30-minute walk each morning before eating to burn through your glycogen stores, so you start burning fat instead.
- Start calculating your macros and try to stay between 70% and 80% fat, up to 20% protein, and no more than 5% carbohydrates.
- Begin testing your urine for ketones after 4 to 5 days and make adjustments to your diet as needed to fully enter ketosis.

Once your body enters ketosis, all you have to do is maintain it! You don't have to count calories, but you do need to stick to your macros. Don't be tempted to "cheat" with a high-carb day because you could kick yourself out of ketosis and have to start all over. Do what it takes to stay as close to your macro range as possible.

Now that you have a better understanding of what the ketogenic diet is, you may be wondering how the Instant Pot fits in.

The Instant Pot is an electric, programmable pressure cooker that takes the hassle and lengthy prep work out of cooking a delicious and satisfying meal for your family. But what are the benefits of the Instant Pot?

Here's a quick overview of what you can look forward to with your Instant Pot:

- Shorter cook times
- More nutritious food
- Unbeatable flavor
- Energy-efficient cooking
- Easy clean-up

The first benefit on this list highlights the convenience factor that makes the Instant Pot so popular. Pressure cooking involves heating liquid (such as water or broth) to such a point that it turns to steam and that steam creates pressure inside the cooker. As a result, foods cook up to 70% faster while still retaining their natural moisture.

In addition to faster cook times, the Instant Pot yields meals that are more nutritious and flavorful than any other cooking method. With pressure cooking, the heat id evenly and quickly distributed, and the food only stays in the pot for a short amount of time – this means that fewer nutrients are lost during cooking. It also means more flavor!

Aside from the benefits of delicious and nutritious food, pressure cooking is also an energy-efficient and practical cooking method. You use much less energy than you would heating your entire stove, and the cleanup is easy – you simply remove the insert and pop it in the dishwasher or wash by hand.

Doesn't all of that sound amazing?

At this point, you're probably eager to get started in using your Instant Pot. Before you do, here's a quick overview of what you'll find in the coming pages:

- A collection of 70 recipes for breakfast, main meals, side dishes, and desserts
- Delicious and indulgent recipes that adhere to the ketogenic diet
- Simple, easy-to-prepare recipes, most with just 6 main ingredients or less
- Detailed instructions for using the Instant Pot that are easy to follow

If all of that sounds good to you, then don't delay any longer! Start looking through the recipes provided in this book to see which one you want to try first!

Best of luck to you with your new Instant Pot!

Breakfast Recipes

Mexican Egg Casserole

Servings: 8

Prep Time: 5 minutes

Cook Time: 25 minutes

Ingredients:

- 1 pound ground pork sausage
- 1 small yellow onion, chopped
- 8 large eggs
- ¼ cup coconut flour
- 1 cup diced red peppers
- 1 ½ cups shredded Mexican blend cheese

Instructions:

1. Turn the Instant Pot on to the Sauté setting and let it heat up.
2. Add the sausage and onion and cook until the sausage is browned, about 5 minutes.
3. Whisk together the eggs and coconut flour then pour into the pot.
4. Stir in the chopped peppers and Mexican cheese then close and lock the lid.
5. Press the Manual button and adjust the timer to 20 minutes.
6. When the timer goes off, let the pressure vent naturally.
7. When the pot has depressurized, open the lid.
8. Remove the casserole to a plate and let rest 5 minutes before serving.

Nutrition: 375 calories, 28g fat, 23g protein, 7g carbs, 3g fiber, 4g net carbs

Sausage Gravy

Servings: 6

Prep Time: 5 minutes

Cook Time: 5 minutes

Ingredients:

- 1 pound ground pork sausage
- ½ cup chicken broth
- 3 cups whole milk
- 6 tablespoons coconut flour
- Salt and pepper

Instructions:

1. Turn the Instant Pot on to the Sauté setting and let it heat up.
2. Add the sausage and cook until browned, breaking it up into pieces.
3. Pour in the chicken broth then close and lock the lid.
4. Press the Manual button and adjust the timer to 5 minutes.
5. When the timer goes off, do a Quick Release by pressing Cancel and switching the steam valve to "venting".
6. When the pot has depressurized, open the lid.
7. Whisk together the milk and coconut flour then stir into the pot.
8. Cook on Sauté mode for 5 minutes until the sausage is thick.
9. Season with salt and pepper then serve over keto biscuits.

Nutrition: 375 calories, 26g fat, 20g protein, 13.5g carbs, 5g fiber, 8.5g net carbs

Sausage and Broccoli Egg Casserole

Servings: 6

Prep Time: 10 minutes

Cook Time: 35 minutes

Ingredients:

- 1 tablespoon olive oil
- 8 ounces ground breakfast sausage
- 1 ½ cups grated broccoli
- 2 cloves minced garlic
- 6 large eggs
- ¼ cup heavy cream
- 1 cup shredded cheddar cheese

Instructions:

1. Turn the Instant Pot on to the Sauté setting and let it heat up.
2. Meanwhile grease a small casserole dish that can fit in the pot using cooking spray.
3. Heat the oil then add the sausage and cook until browned, about 5 minutes, breaking it up with a spoon.
4. Stir in the grated broccoli and garlic then season with salt and pepper.
5. Cook for 2 to 3 minutes then spoon the mixture into the casserole dish.
6. Whisk together the eggs, cream, and cheese then pour into the casserole dish.
7. Cover the dish with foil and place it in the pot on top of a trivet.
8. Pour in one cup of water then close and lock the lid.
9. Press the Manual button and adjust the timer to 35 minutes.
10. When the timer goes off, let the pressure vent for 10 minutes then do a Quick Release by pressing Cancel and switching the steam valve to "venting".
11. When the pot has depressurized, open the lid.

12. Remove the casserole from the pot and let it rest for 10 minutes before slicing.

Nutrition: 315 calories, 25.5g fat, 18.5g protein, 2.5g carbs, 0.5g fiber, 2g net carbs

Burrito Breakfast Bowl

Servings: 4

Prep Time: 5 minutes

Cook Time: 10 minutes

Ingredients:

- 2 tablespoons butter
- 6 large eggs
- 8 ounces breakfast sausage links, cooked and sliced
- ½ cup shredded cheddar cheese
- ½ cup sour cream
- 1 cup diced avocado

Instructions:

1. Turn the Instant Pot on to the Sauté setting and let it heat up.
2. Add the butter and let it melt.
3. Add the eggs to the pot and cook for 5 to 6 minutes, stirring gently, until they start to firm up.
4. Stir in the sausage and cheese and cook until the eggs are done.
5. Press the Cancel button to turn off the pot.
6. Spoon the egg mixture into four bowls.
7. Top with diced avocado and sour cream to serve.

Nutrition: 420 calories, 34g fat, 22.5g protein, 8g carbs, 2.5g fiber, 5.5g net carbs

Easy Eggs in a Jar

Servings: 4

Prep Time: 5 minutes

Cook Time: 5 minutes

Ingredients:

- 4 large eggs
- ½ cup diced yellow onion
- ½ cup diced mushrooms
- ½ cup shredded cheddar cheese
- ¼ cup heavy cream
- Salt and pepper

Instructions:

1. Whisk together the eggs, onions, mushrooms, cheese, and heavy cream in a bowl.
2. Season with salt and pepper then pour into four ½-pint jars.
3. Place the lids loosely on top of the jars and place them in the Instant Pot on a trivet.
4. Pour in 2 cups of water then close and lock the lid.
5. Press the Manual button and adjust the timer to 5 minutes on High Pressure.
6. When the timer goes off, do a Quick Release by pressing Cancel and switching the steam valve to "venting".
7. When the pot has depressurized, open the lid.
8. Remove the jars from the Instant Pot and serve the eggs immediately.

Nutrition: 165 calories, 12.5g fat, 10.5g protein, 2.5g carbs, 0.5g fiber, 2g net carbs

Cheesy Cauliflower and Ham Casserole

Servings: 6

Prep Time: 5 minutes

Cook Time: 30 minutes

Ingredients:

- 1 tablespoon olive oil
- 8 ounces diced ham
- 1 ½ cups grated cauliflower
- 2 cloves minced garlic
- 6 large eggs
- ¼ cup heavy cream
- 1 cup shredded mozzarella cheese

Instructions:

1. Turn the Instant Pot on to the Sauté setting and let it heat up.
2. Meanwhile, grease a small casserole dish that can fit in the pot using cooking spray.
3. Heat the oil then add the grated cauliflower and garlic - season with salt and pepper.
4. Cook for 2 to 3 minutes then stir in the diced ham and spoon the mixture into the casserole dish.
5. Whisk together the eggs, cream, and cheese then pour into the casserole dish.
6. Cover the dish with foil and place it in the pot on top of a trivet.
7. Pour in one cup of water then close and lock the lid.
8. Press the Manual button and adjust the timer to 30 minutes.
9. When the timer goes off, let the pressure vent for 10 minutes then do a Quick Release by pressing Cancel and switching the steam valve to "venting".
10. When the pot has depressurized, open the lid.

11. Remove the casserole from the pot and let it rest for 10 minutes before slicing.

Nutrition: 190 calories, 13g fat, 14.5g protein, 4g carbs, 1g fiber, 3g net carbs

Easy Spinach and Tomato Frittata

Servings: 4

Prep Time: 5 minutes

Cook Time: 5 minutes

Ingredients:

- 6 large eggs
- 1 cup fresh chopped spinach
- ½ cup diced tomatoes
- 2 tablespoons diced yellow onion
- ½ teaspoon garlic powder
- Salt and pepper

Instructions:

1. Whisk together all of the ingredients.
2. Pour the mixture into a greased 7-inch springform pan.
3. Place the pan in the Instant Pot on top of a trivet.
4. Pour in 1 cup of water then close and lock the lid.
5. Press the Manual button and adjust the timer to 5 minutes.
6. When the timer goes off, let the pressure vent for 10 minutes then do a Quick Release by pressing Cancel and switching the steam valve to "venting".
7. When the pot has depressurized, open the lid.
8. Remove the pan from the pot and let the frittata rest for 5 minutes before serving.

Nutrition: 115 calories, 7.5g fat, 10g protein, 2.5g carbs, 0.5g fiber, 2g net carbs

Bacon, Cheese, and Veggie Egg Bake

Servings: 4

Prep Time: 10 minutes

Cook Time: 20 minutes

Ingredients:

- 6 slices bacon, chopped
- 1 cup chopped cauliflower
- ½ cup diced mushrooms
- 6 large eggs
- ¼ cup heavy cream
- ½ cup shredded cheddar cheese
- Salt and pepper

Instructions:

1. Turn the Instant Pot on to the Sauté setting and let it heat up.
2. Add the bacon and cook until crisp.
3. Stir in the vegetables and cook for 3 minutes, stirring often, until tender.
4. Grease a heatproof bowl with cooking spray.
5. Whisk together the eggs, cheese, and cream then season with salt and pepper.
6. Pour the egg mixture into the greased bowl then stir in the bacon and veggies.
7. Place the bowl in the pot on top of a trivet and pour in 1 ½ cups water.
8. Close and lock the lid then press the Manual button and adjust the timer to 20 minutes.
9. When the timer goes off, do a Quick Release by pressing Cancel and switching the steam valve to "venting".
10. When the pot has depressurized, open the lid.
11. Remove the bowl and turn the egg bake out and slice to serve.

Nutrition: 275 calories, 21g fat, 19g protein, 3g carbs, 1g fiber, 2g net carbs

Mediterranean-Style Frittata

Servings: 4

Prep Time: 5 minutes

Cook Time: 5 minutes

Ingredients:

- 6 large eggs
- 1 cup fresh chopped spinach
- ½ cup diced tomatoes
- ½ cup feta cheese, crumbled
- ¼ cup sliced black olives
- ½ teaspoon dried Italian seasoning
- Salt and pepper

Instructions:

1. Whisk together all of the ingredients.
2. Pour the mixture into a greased pan that fits in the pot.
3. Place the pan in the Instant Pot on top of a trivet.
4. Pour in 1 cup of water then close and lock the lid.
5. Press the Manual button and adjust the timer to 5 minutes.
6. When the timer goes off, let the pressure vent for 10 minutes then do a Quick Release by pressing Cancel and switching the steam valve to "venting".
7. When the pot has depressurized, open the lid.
8. Remove the pan from the pot and let the frittata rest for 5 minutes before serving.

Nutrition: 175 calories, 12.5g fat, 12.5g protein, 3g carbs, 1g fiber, 2g net carbs

Cheddar, Ham, and Chive Egg Cups

Servings: 4

Prep Time: 5 minutes

Cook Time: 5 minutes

Ingredients:

- 4 large eggs
- ½ cup diced yellow onion
- ½ cup diced ham
- 2 tablespoons chopped chives
- ½ cup shredded cheddar cheese
- ¼ cup heavy cream
- Salt and pepper

Instructions:

1. Whisk together the eggs, onions, ham, cheese, chives, and heavy cream in a bowl.
2. Season with salt and pepper then pour into four ½-pint jars.
3. Place the lids loosely on top of the jars and place them in the Instant Pot on a trivet.
4. Pour in 2 cups of water then close and lock the lid.
5. Press the Manual button and adjust the timer to 5 minutes on High Pressure.
6. When the timer goes off, do a Quick Release by pressing Cancel and switching the steam valve to "venting".
7. When the pot has depressurized, open the lid.
8. Remove the jars from the Instant Pot and serve the eggs immediately.

Nutrition: 190 calories, 14g fat, 13g protein, 3g carbs, 0.5g fiber, 2.5g net carbs

Fish and Seafood Recipes

Easy Lemon Pepper Salmon

Servings: 4

Prep Time: 5 minutes

Cook Time: 3 minutes

Ingredients:

- 3 sprigs fresh herbs (your choice)
- 1 pound boneless salmon fillets
- Salt and pepper
- 1 tablespoon olive oil
- ½ lemon, sliced thin

Instructions:

1. Pour ¾ cup of water in the Instant Pot and add the herbs.
2. Place the steamer rack in the pot and place the salmon on it, skin-side-down.
3. Season with salt and pepper then drizzle with oil and layer with lemon slices.
4. Close and lock the lid.
5. Press the Steam button and adjust the timer to 3 minutes.
6. When the timer goes off, do a Quick Release by pressing Cancel and switching the steam valve to "venting".
7. When the pot has depressurized, open the lid.
8. Remove the salmon to a plate and serve immediately.

Nutrition: 180 calories, 10.5g fat, 22g protein, 0g carbs, 0g fiber, 0g net carbs

Lobster Bisque

Servings: 8

Prep Time: 5 minutes

Cook Time: 4 minutes

Ingredients:

- 2 tablespoons butter
- 1 small yellow onion, chopped
- 2 (14-ounce) cans diced tomatoes
- 4 cups chicken broth
- 1 tablespoon Old Bay seasoning
- 24 ounces fresh lobster tails
- 2 cups heavy cream

Instructions:

1. Turn the Instant Pot on to the Sauté setting and let it heat up.
2. Add the butter and let it melt then sauté the onions for 3 minutes.
3. Stir in the diced tomatoes, chicken broth, and Old Bay seasoning.
4. Add the lobster tails and season with salt and pepper.
5. Close and lock the lid then press the Manual button and adjust the timer to 4 minutes.
6. When the timer goes off, let the pressure vent naturally.
7. When the pot has depressurized, open the lid.
8. Remove the lobster tails and separate the meat. Chop it coarsely then add it back to the pot.
9. Stir in the cream then adjust seasoning to taste and serve hot.

Nutrition: 245 calories, 15.5g fat, 20g protein, 6g carbs, 1.5g fiber, 4.5g net carbs

Shrimp Scampi

Servings: 6

Prep Time: 5 minutes

Cook Time: 1 minutes

Ingredients:

- ¼ cup butter
- 3 cloves minced garlic
- ½ cup dry white wine
- ½ cup chicken broth
- 2 pounds large shrimp, peeled and deveined
- 1 tablespoon fresh lemon juice
- Salt and pepper

Instructions:

1. Turn the Instant Pot on to the Sauté setting and let it heat up.
2. Add the butter and garlic then cook for 1 minute, stirring.
3. Pour in the wine and cook for a minute or two before adding the chicken broth.
4. Add the shrimp then close and lock the lid.
5. Press the Meat/Stew button and adjust the timer to 1 minute.
6. When the timer goes off, let the pressure vent for 5 minutes then do a Quick Release by pressing Cancel and switching the steam valve to "venting".
7. When the pot has depressurized, open the lid.
8. Stir in the lemon juice then season with salt and pepper and serve hot.

Nutrition: 215 calories, 8g fat, 29g protein, 4g carbs, 0g fiber, 4g net carbs

Coconut Fish Curry

Servings: 6

Prep Time: 10 minutes

Cook Time: 5 minutes

Ingredients:

- 1 tablespoon coconut oil
- 1 small yellow onion, diced
- 1 tablespoon fresh grated ginger
- 2 cups unsweetened coconut milk
- 1 tablespoon curry powder
- 1 medium tomato, diced
- 1 ½ pounds white fish fillet, cut into 2-inch pieces

Instructions:

1. Press the Sauté button on the Instant Pot and let it heat up.
2. Add the oil then stir in the onion and ginger – cook for 2 minutes.
3. Stir in the coconut milk and curry powder then cook for 1 minute more.
4. Add the diced tomatoes and fish, stirring to coat, then close and lock the lid.
5. Press the Manual button and adjust the timer to 5 minutes on Low Pressure.
6. When the timer goes off, do a Quick Release by pressing Cancel and switching the steam valve to "venting".
7. When the pot has depressurized, open the lid.
8. Adjust the seasoning to taste then serve hot.

Nutrition: 245 calories, 12.5g fat, 28g protein, 4g carbs, 1.5g fiber, 2.5g net carbs

Ginger Soy Salmon

Servings: 4

Prep Time: 5 minutes

Cook Time: 3 minutes

Ingredients:

- 2 tablespoons fresh orange juice
- 2 tablespoons soy sauce
- 1 tablespoon fresh grated ginger
- 2 cloves minced garlic
- 1 pound boneless salmon fillet
- Salt and pepper

Instructions:

1. Place the steamer rack in the Instant Pot and add 2 cups of water.
2. Whisk together the orange juice, soy sauce, ginger, and garlic in a large zippered freezer bag.
3. Season the salmon with salt and pepper then add to the bag.
4. Shake to coat then marinate for 30 minutes. Place the bag in the Instant Pot on top of the steamer rack then close and lock the lid.
5. Press the Manual button and adjust the timer to 3 minutes on Low Pressure.
6. When the timer goes off, let the pressure vent for 5 minutes then do a Quick Release by pressing Cancel and switching the steam valve to "venting".
7. When the pot has depressurized, open the lid.
8. Transfer the salmon to a roasting pan and broil for 3 minutes. Serve hot.

Nutrition: 165 calories, 7g fat, 23g protein, 3g carbs, 0.5g fiber, 2.5g net carbs

Steamed Mussels

Servings: 4

Prep Time: 5 minutes

Cook Time: 5 minutes

Ingredients:

- 2 pounds live mussels
- 2 tablespoons butter
- 1 small yellow onion, chopped
- 2 cloves minced garlic
- ¾ cup chicken broth
- ¼ cup white wine

Instructions:

1. Rinse the mussels well and clean them, discarding any that are open.
2. Turn the Instant Pot on to the Sauté function and let it heat up.
3. Melt the butter then add the onions and garlic, cooking for 3 minutes.
4. Stir in the chicken broth and wine then scrape up any browned bits.
5. Add the mussels then close and lock the lid.
6. Press the Manual button and adjust the timer to 5 minutes.
7. When the timer goes off, let the pressure vent naturally.
8. When the pot has depressurized, open the lid.
9. Spoon the mussels into bowls using a slotted spoon and serve with melted butter.

Nutrition: 280 calories, 11g fat, 28g protein, 11.5g carbs, 0.5g fiber, 10g net carbs

Lemon Tilapia Packets

Servings: 4

Prep Time: 5 minutes

Cook Time: 8 minutes

Ingredients:

- 4 (6-ounce) tilapia fillets, boneless
- 2 tablespoons olive oil
- ½ teaspoon paprika
- Salt and pepper
- 4 slices lemon

Instructions:

1. Place the steamer rack in the Instant Pot and add 1 ½ cups of water.
2. Cut out four pieces of parchment paper and place a tilapia fillet on each.
3. Brush the fillets with oil then season with paprika, salt, and pepper.
4. Top each fillet with a slice of lemon then fold the parchment paper into packets.
5. Place the packets on the steamer insert then close and lock the lid.
6. Press the Manual button and adjust the timer to 8 minutes.
7. When the timer goes off, do a Quick Release by pressing Cancel and switching the steam valve to "venting".
8. When the pot has depressurized, open the lid.
9. Remove the packets and serve the fish immediately.

Nutrition: 250 calories, 13g fat, 31g protein, 1g carbs, 1g fiber, 1g net carbs

Steamed Crab Legs

Servings: 4

Prep Time: 5 minutes

Cook Time: 3 minutes

Ingredients:

- 2 pounds crab legs
- ½ cup butter, melted

Instructions:

1. Place the steamer rack in the Instant Pot and add 1 cup of water.
2. Add the crab legs to the pot then close and lock the lid.
3. Press the Manual button and adjust the timer to 3 minutes.
4. When the timer goes off, do a Quick Release by pressing Cancel and switching the steam valve to "venting".
5. When the pot has depressurized, open the lid.
6. Remove the crab legs to a platter using tongs and serve with melted butter.

Nutrition: 315 calories, 25g fat, 21.5g protein, 0g carbs, 0g fiber, 0g net carbs

Coconut Shrimp

Servings: 4

Prep Time: 10 minutes

Cook Time: 5 minutes

Ingredients:

- 1 pound large shrimp, peeled and deveined
- ¾ cup canned coconut milk
- 1 tablespoon fresh grated ginger
- 1 tablespoon minced garlic
- 1 teaspoon turmeric
- Pinch cayenne

Instructions:

1. Place the steamer rack in the Instant Pot and add 2 cups of water.
2. Whisk together the coconut milk, ginger, garlic, turmeric, and cayenne in a bowl.
3. Toss in the shrimp then transfer to a heatproof bowl and cover with foil.
4. Place the bowl in the Instant Pot on top of the trivet then close and lock the lid.
5. Press the Manual button and adjust the timer to 4 minutes on Low Pressure.
6. When the timer goes off, do a Quick Release by pressing Cancel and switching the steam valve to "venting".
7. When the pot has depressurized, open the lid and remove the bowl to serve.

Nutrition: 205 calories, 11g fat, 22.5g protein, 6.5g carbs, 1.5g fiber, 5g net carbs

Chili Lime Salmon

Servings: 4

Prep Time: 5 minutes

Cook Time: 5 minutes

Ingredients:

- 4 (6-ounce) boneless salmon fillets
- Salt and pepper
- 2 limes, juiced
- 2 tablespoons olive oil
- 2 jalapenos, seeded and minced
- 2 cloves minced garlic
- 1 teaspoon paprika

Instructions:

1. Place the steamer rack in the Instant Pot and add 1 cup of water.
2. Season the salmon with salt and pepper then place it on the steamer rack.
3. Close and lock the lid then press the Steam button and adjust the timer to 5 minutes.
4. When the timer goes off, do a Quick Release by pressing Cancel and switching the steam valve to "venting".
5. When the pot has depressurized, open the lid.
6. Whisk together the lime juice, olive oil, jalapeno, garlic, and paprika in a bowl.
7. Remove the salmon from the pot and drizzle with the glaze to serve.

Nutrition: 295 calories, 17.5g fat, 33.5g protein, 3g carbs, 0.5g fiber, 2.5g net carbs

Poultry Recipes

Indian Butter Chicken

Servings: 4

Prep Time: 10 minutes

Cook Time: 10 minutes

Ingredients:

- 1 tablespoon olive oil
- 1 small yellow onion, chopped
- 1 pound boneless chicken thighs, chopped
- 1 (14-ounce) can diced tomatoes
- 1 ½ teaspoons ground coriander
- 1 teaspoon ground turmeric
- ½ cup heavy cream

Instructions:

1. Turn the Instant Pot on to the Sauté setting and let it heat up.
2. Add the olive oil then cook the onions until browned.
3. Stir in the chicken, diced tomatoes, and seasonings.
4. Close and lock the lid then press the Manual button and adjust the timer to 10 minutes.
5. When the timer goes off, let the pressure vent for 10 minutes then do a Quick Release by pressing Cancel and switching the steam valve to "venting".
6. When the pot has depressurized, open the lid.
7. Use a slotted spoon to remove the chicken the puree the sauce in the pot.
8. Stir in the heavy cream and the cooked chicken. Serve hot.

Nutrition: 350 calories, 26g fat, 21.5g protein, 6g carbs, 1.5g fiber, 4.5g net carbs

Turkey-Stuffed Peppers

Servings: 4

Prep Time: 10 minutes

Cook Time: 15 minutes

Ingredients:

- 4 small red bell peppers
- 1 pound ground turkey (85% lean)
- ½ small yellow onion, diced
- ¼ cup grated parmesan cheese
- ½ cup low-carb tomato sauce
- 1 large egg
- Salt and pepper
- ½ cup water

Instructions:

1. Slice the tops off the peppers and remove the pith.
2. Stir together the ground turkey, onion, and parmesan cheese in a bowl.
3. Add the tomato sauce and egg then season with salt and pepper.
4. Spoon the mixture into the peppers.
5. Place the steamer insert in the Instant Pot and place the peppers in it.
6. Add the water then close and lock the lid.
7. Press the Manual button and adjust the timer to 15 minutes.
8. When the timer goes off, let the pressure vent naturally.
9. When the pot has depressurized, open the lid, and remove the peppers.

Nutrition: 380 calories, 24g fat, 29g protein, 10.5g carbs, 2g fiber, 8.5g net carbs

Garlic Soy-Glazed Chicken

Servings: 6

Prep Time: 20 minutes

Cook Time: 15 minutes

Ingredients:

- 2 pounds boneless chicken thighs
- Salt and pepper
- ¾ cup apple cider vinegar
- ¼ cup soy sauce
- 1 tablespoon minced garlic

Instructions:

1. Season the chicken with salt and pepper then add it to the Instant Pot, skin-side down.
2. Whisk together the apple cider vinegar, soy sauce, and garlic then add to the pot.
3. Close and lock the lid then press the Manual button and adjust the timer to 15 minutes.
4. When the timer goes off, let the pressure vent naturally.
5. When the pot has depressurized, open the lid.
6. Remove the chicken to a baking sheet and place under the broiler for 3 to 5 minutes until the skin is crisp.
7. Meanwhile, turn the Instant Pot on to Sauté and cook until the sauce thickens, stirring as needed.
8. Serve the chicken with the sauce spooned over it.

Nutrition: 335 calories, 23g fat, 27.5g protein, 1.5g carbs, 0g fiber, 1.5g net carbs

Italian Turkey Breast with Gravy

Servings: 8

Prep Time: 25 minutes

Cook Time: 25 minutes

Ingredients:

- 3 tablespoons butter, divided
- 1 (4-pound) bone-in turkey breast
- 1 tablespoon Italian seasoning
- Salt and pepper
- 1 tablespoon coconut flour
- ½ cup chicken broth
- ½ cup whole milk

Instructions:

1. Turn the Instant Pot on to the Sauté setting and let it heat up.
2. Rub 1 tablespoon of the butter into the turkey breast and season with Italian seasoning, salt, and pepper.
3. Add the turkey to the Instant Pot and cook for 2 minutes on each side to brown.
4. Remove the turkey and place the steamer insert in the pot.
5. Add the turkey to the steamer insert then close and lock the lid.
6. Press the Manual button and adjust the timer to 25 minutes.
7. When the timer goes off, let the pressure vent naturally.
8. When the pot has depressurized, open the lid.
9. Remove the turkey to a cutting board and tent loosely with foil.
10. Add the remaining butter to the pot and whisk in the coconut flour.
11. Press the Sauté button and simmer the sauce for 2 minutes.
12. Whisk in the chicken broth and milk then cook until thickened, about 3 minutes.
13. Slice the turkey breast and serve with the gravy.

Nutrition: 440 calories, 21g fat, 49g protein, 2g carbs, 1g fiber, 1g net carbs

Whole Roasted Chicken

Servings: 8

Prep Time: 15 minutes

Cook Time: 24 minutes

Ingredients:

- 2 tablespoons butter
- 1 (4-pound) whole roasting chicken
- 2 teaspoons paprika
- Salt and pepper
- 1 small onion, quartered
- 1 lemon, halved
- 1 cup water

Instructions:

1. Turn the Instant Pot on to the Sauté setting and let it heat up.
2. Rub the butter into the chicken then season with paprika, salt, and pepper.
3. Place the onion and lemon in the chicken cavity.
4. Add the chicken to the preheated instant pot, skin-side down, and cook for 6 to 7 minutes until browned.
5. Turn the chicken and cook for another 5 minutes then remove from the pot.
6. Place the trivet inside the Instant Pot and pour in the water.
7. Place the chicken on the trivet then close and lock the lid.
8. Press the Manual button and adjust the timer to 24 minutes.
9. When the timer goes off, let the pressure vent for 15 minutes then do a Quick Release by pressing Cancel and switching the steam valve to "venting".
10. When the pot has depressurized, open the lid.
11. Remove the chicken to a cutting board and let rest 10 minutes before carving.

Nutrition: 490 calories, 35g fat, 43g protein, 2.5g carbs, 0.5g fiber, 2g net carbs

Italian Chicken Stew

Servings: 4

Prep Time: 10 minutes

Cook Time: 10 minutes

Ingredients:

- 1 tablespoon olive oil
- 1 small yellow onion, chopped
- 1 (14-ounce) can diced tomatoes
- 1 ½ cups chicken broth
- 1 tablespoon tomato paste
- 1 teaspoon dried Italian seasoning
- 12 ounces boneless chicken thighs

Instructions:

1. Turn the Instant Pot on to the Sauté setting and let it heat up.
2. Add the olive oil then sauté the onion for 5 minutes until softened.
3. Add the tomatoes, chicken broth, tomato paste, and seasoning.
4. Stir well then add the chicken and close and lock the lid.
5. Press the Manual button and adjust the timer to 10 minutes on High Pressure.
6. When the timer goes off, let the pressure vent for 10 minutes then do a Quick Release by pressing Cancel and switching the steam valve to "venting".
7. When the pot has depressurized, open the lid.
8. Remove the chicken with a slotted spoon and shred it with two forks.
9. Simmer the cooking liquid on the Sauté setting until it thickens then stir the chicken back in to serve.

Nutrition: 255 calories, 17.5g fat, 18g protein, 6.5g carbs, 1.5g fiber, 5g net carbs

Chicken Cacciatore

Servings: 4

Prep Time: 5 minutes

Cook Time: 15 minutes

Ingredients:

- 1 tablespoon olive oil
- 1 ½ pounds boneless chicken thighs, chopped
- 1 (14-ounce) can stewed tomatoes
- 1 small yellow onion, chopped
- 2 cloves minced garlic
- 1 teaspoon dried oregano
- ½ cup sliced black olives

Instructions:

1. Turn the Instant Pot on to the Sauté setting and let it heat up with the oil.
2. Add the chicken and sauté for 3 to 4 minutes until browned.
3. Stir in the tomatoes, onions, garlic, and oregano.
4. Close and lock the lid then press the Manual button and adjust the timer to 15 minutes.
5. When the timer goes off, let the pressure vent naturally.
6. When the pot has depressurized, open the lid.
7. Stir in the olives and season with salt and pepper. Serve hot.

Nutrition: 440 calories, 31g fat, 31g protein, 7g carbs, 2g fiber, 5g net carbs

Stewed Chicken and Kale

Servings: 4

Prep Time: 5 minutes

Cook Time: 10 minutes

Ingredients:

- 1 tablespoon butter
- 1 small yellow onion, chopped
- 1 pound boneless chicken thighs, chopped
- 1 (14-ounce) can diced tomatoes
- 1 cup chicken broth
- 3 cups fresh chopped kale
- Salt and pepper

Instructions:

1. Turn the Instant Pot on to the Sauté setting and let it heat up.
2. Melt the butter in the pot then add the onion.
3. Cook for 3 minutes to soften then stir in the chicken.
4. Add the tomatoes, chicken broth, and kale then season with salt and pepper.
5. Close and lock the lid.
6. Press the Manual button and adjust the timer to 10 minutes.
7. When the timer goes off, let the pressure vent for 10 minutes then do a Quick Release by pressing Cancel and switching the steam valve to "venting".
8. When the pot has depressurized, open the lid.
9. Stir everything together and adjust seasoning to taste.

Nutrition: 325 calories, 20.5g fat, 24g protein, 11g carbs, 2.5g fiber, 8.5g net carbs

Lemon Garlic Chicken

Servings: 8

Prep Time: 10 minutes

Cook Time: 7 minutes

Ingredients:

- 2 tablespoons olive oil
- 2 pounds boneless chicken thighs
- Salt and pepper
- 1 small yellow onion, chopped
- 3 cloves minced garlic
- ½ cup fresh lemon juice
- ¼ cup heavy cream

Instructions:

1. Turn the Instant Pot on to the Sauté setting and let it heat up.
2. Heat the oil in the pot then add the chicken – season with salt and pepper.
3. Cook to brown the chicken, about 2 to 3 minutes on each side.
4. Remove the chicken from the pot and add the onion, and garlic.
5. Stir in the lemon juice and cook for 1 minute.
6. Add the chicken back to the pot then close and lock the lid.
7. Press the Manual button and adjust the timer to 7 minutes.
8. When the timer goes off, let the pressure vent for 5 minutes then do a Quick Release by pressing Cancel and switching the steam valve to "venting".
9. When the pot has depressurized, open the lid.
10. Remove the chicken from the pot and stir in the cream.
11. Cook on the Sauté function for 2 to 3 minutes until thickened.
12. Spoon the sauce over the chicken to serve.

Nutrition: 300 calories, 22g fat, 20.5g protein, 1.5g carbs, 0.5g fiber, 1g net carbs

Creamy Salsa Chicken

Servings: 6

Prep Time: 5 minutes

Cook Time: 20 minutes

Ingredients:

- 2 pounds boneless chicken thighs
- 1 tablespoon ground cumin
- 1 tablespoon ground coriander
- Salt and pepper
- 1 cup salsa
- ¼ cup chicken broth
- 4 ounces cream cheese, chopped

Instructions:

1. Season the chicken with the cumin, coriander, salt, and pepper.
2. Add the chicken to the Instant Pot with the salsa, chicken broth, and cream cheese.
3. Close and lock the lid.
4. Press the Manual button and adjust the timer to 20 minutes on High Pressure.
5. When the timer goes off, let the pressure vent for 15 minutes then do a Quick Release by pressing Cancel and switching the steam valve to "venting".
6. When the pot has depressurized, open the lid.
7. Shred the chicken with two forks and stir everything well. Serve hot.

Nutrition: 400 calories, 29.5g fat, 29g protein, 3g carbs, 0.5g fiber, 2.5g net carbs

Beef Recipes

Easy Beef Bourguignon

Servings: 6

Prep Time: 10 minutes

Cook Time: 30 minutes

Ingredients:

- 1 ½ tablespoons olive oil
- 1 pound beef stew meat, chopped
- Salt and pepper
- 8 slices bacon, chopped
- 1 small yellow onion, chopped
- 3 cloves minced garlic
- 1 ½ cups beef broth

Instructions:

1. Turn the Instant Pot on to the Sauté setting and let it heat up.
2. Add the oil then season the beef with salt and pepper and add it to the pot.
3. Cook for 4 to 5 minutes until browned, stirring often.
4. Add the bacon, onions, and garlic and cook for 4 minutes, stirring.
5. Stir in the beef broth then season with salt and pepper.
6. Close and lock the lid on the Instant Pot.
7. Press the Manual button and adjust the timer to 30 minutes.
8. When the timer goes off, let the pressure vent naturally.
9. When the pot has depressurized, open the lid.
10. Stir well and adjust seasoning to taste. Serve hot.

Nutrition: 255 calories, 14g fat, 29g protein, 2g carbs, 0.5g fiber, 1.5g net carbs

Shredded Beef

Servings: 6

Prep Time: 15 minutes

Cook Time: 1 hour 15 minutes

Ingredients:

- 2 tablespoons olive oil
- 3 pounds boneless beef rump roast
- Salt and pepper
- 1 ¼ cups beef broth
- 1 teaspoon dried oregano
- 1 teaspoon dried thyme
- 1 teaspoon dried basil

Instructions:

1. Turn the Instant Pot on to the Sauté setting and let it heat up.
2. Add the oil to the pot and season the beef with salt and pepper.
3. Add the beef and cook for 2 minutes on each side until browned.
4. Whisk together the remaining ingredients and pour into the pot with the beef.
5. Close and lock the lid.
6. Press the Manual button and adjust the timer to 75 minutes.
7. When the timer goes off, let the pressure vent naturally. When the pot has depressurized, open the lid.
8. Shred the beef with two forks and stir into the cooking liquid.

Nutrition: 455 calories, 18.5g fat, 71.5g protein, 0.5g carbs, 0g fiber, 0.5g net carbs

Braised Beef Short Ribs

Servings: 8

Prep Time: 15 minutes

Cook Time: 35 minutes

Ingredients:

- 1 tablespoon olive oil
- 2 pounds boneless beef short ribs
- Salt and pepper
- 1 small yellow onion, chopped
- ½ cup red wine
- ¼ cup tomato paste
- 1 tablespoon Worcestershire sauce

Instructions:

1. Turn the Instant Pot on to the Sauté setting and let it heat up.
2. Add the oil to the pot and season the short ribs with salt and pepper.
3. Place the ribs in the pot and cook for 2 minutes on each side to brown.
4. Remove the ribs then add the onions to the pot and cook for 5 minutes.
5. Stir in the garlic then add the rest of the ingredients, including the ribs.
6. Close and lock the lid then press the Manual button and adjust the timer to 35 minutes.
7. When the timer goes off, let the pressure vent for 5 minutes then do a Quick Release by pressing Cancel and switching the steam valve to "venting".
8. When the pot has depressurized, open the lid. Remove the ribs to serve.

Nutrition: 480 calories, 43g fat, 16.5g protein, 3g carbs, 0.5g fiber, 2.5g net carbs

Classic Meatloaf

Servings: 8

Prep Time: 10 minutes

Cook Time: 35 minutes

Ingredients:

- 2 pounds ground beef (80% lean)
- 1 cup almond flour
- 1 cup grated parmesan cheese
- 3 large eggs
- 1 tablespoon minced garlic
- 1 teaspoon dried oregano
- Salt and pepper

Instructions:

1. Combine the ground beef, almond flour, parmesan cheese, eggs, garlic, and oregano in a bowl.
2. Mix well by hand then season with salt and pepper.
3. Place the steamer rack in your Instant Pot and line with foil.
4. Shape the meat mixture into a loaf and place it on the foil, close and lock the lid.
5. Press the Manual button and adjust the timer to 35 minutes.
6. When the timer goes off, do a Quick Release by pressing Cancel and switching the steam valve to "venting".
7. When the pot has depressurized, open the lid.
8. Remove the meatloaf to a roasting pan and broil for 5 minutes to brown before slicing to serve.

Nutrition: 460 calories, 31g fat, 39.5g protein, 3g carbs, 1.5g fiber

Korean BBQ Beef

Servings: 6

Prep Time: 10 minutes

Cook Time: 15 minutes

Ingredients:

- 1/3 cup soy sauce
- 6 tablespoons powdered erythritol
- 1 tablespoon fresh grated ginger
- 3 cloves minced garlic
- 2 tablespoons rice wine vinegar
- 3 pounds boneless beef chuck roast, cut into chunks
- Salt and pepper

Instructions:

1. Whisk together the soy sauce, powdered erythritol, ginger, garlic, and rice wine vinegar in a bowl.
2. Season the beef with salt and pepper then place it in the Instant Pot.
3. Pour the sauce over it then close and lock the lid.
4. Press the Manual button and adjust the timer to 15 minutes.
5. When the timer goes off, do a Quick Release by pressing Cancel and switching the steam valve to "venting".
6. When the pot has depressurized, open the lid. Serve the beef hot.

Nutrition: 440 calories, 14g fat, 70g protein, 2.5g carbs, 0.5g fiber, 2g net carbs

Bolognese Sauce

Servings: 8

Prep Time: 20 minutes

Cook Time: 20 minutes

Ingredients:

- 1 tablespoon olive oil
- 1 small yellow onion, chopped
- 1 pound ground beef (80% lean)
- ¼ pound chopped bacon
- 2 tablespoons tomato paste
- 2 (14-ounce) cans crushed tomatoes
- ¼ cup heavy cream

Instructions:

1. Turn the Instant Pot on to the Sauté setting and let it heat up.
2. Add the oil to the pot and add the onions – sauté for 4 to 5 minutes.
3. Stir in the beef and bacon then cook until browned, about 10 minutes.
4. Stir in the tomato paste and cook 1 minute more than pour in the wine.
5. Add tomatoes and ½ cup water, bring to a simmer, then close and lock the lid.
6. Press the Manual button and adjust the timer to 20 minutes.
7. When the timer goes off, do a Quick Release by pressing Cancel and switching the steam valve to "venting".
8. When the pot has depressurized, open the lid.
9. Stir in the heavy cream and adjust the seasoning to taste.
10. Press the Sauté button and simmer until the sauce has thickened and serve over zucchini noodles.

Nutrition: 305 calories, 19g fat, 23g protein, 10g carbs, 3.5g fiber, 6.5g net carbs

Stewed Beef with Mushrooms

Servings: 6

Prep Time: 15 minutes

Cook Time: 17 minutes

Ingredients:

- 1 ½ tablespoons olive oil
- 2 pounds beef stew meat, chopped
- Salt and pepper
- 10 ounces sliced mushrooms
- 2 cloves minced garlic
- 2 tablespoons almond flour
- 3 cups beef broth

Instructions:

1. Turn the Instant Pot on to the Sauté setting and let it heat up.
2. Add the oil to the pot and season the beef with salt and pepper.
3. Add the beef to the pot and cook for 4 to 5 minutes until browned.
4. Stir in the mushrooms and garlic and cook for 3 to 4 minutes.
5. Stir in the almond flour and ¼ cup water, scraping up the browned bits.
6. Add the beef broth then close and lock the lid.
7. Press the Manual button and adjust the timer to 5 minutes.
8. When the timer goes off, let the pressure vent for 10 minutes then do a Quick Release by pressing Cancel and switching the steam valve to "venting".
9. When the pot has depressurized, open the lid.
10. Stir everything together well then serve hot.

Nutrition: 355 calories, 15g fat, 50g protein, 3g carbs, 1g fiber, 2g net carbs

Beef and Chorizo Chili

Servings: 6

Prep Time: 10 minutes

Cook Time: 15 minutes

Ingredients:

- 1 tablespoon olive oil
- ½ pound diced chorizo sausage
- 1 small yellow onion, chopped
- 1 pound ground beef (80% lean)
- 3 cloves minced garlic
- Salt and pepper
- 2 cups diced tomatoes

Instructions:

1. Turn the Instant Pot on to the Sauté setting and let it heat up.
2. Add the oil to the pot and season the beef with salt and pepper.
3. Stir in the chorizo and onion and cook for 4 to 5 minutes until the chorizo is browned.
4. Add the beef and garlic then season with salt and pepper – cook for 3 minutes.
5. Stir in the tomatoes then close and lock the lid.
6. Press the Manual button and adjust the timer to 15 minutes.
7. When the timer goes off, let the pressure vent for 5 minutes then do a Quick Release by pressing Cancel and switching the steam valve to "venting".
8. When the pot has depressurized, open the lid. Stir well and serve hot.

Nutrition: 370 calories, 26g fat, 28.5g protein, 4g carbs, 1g fiber, 3g net carbs

Quick and Easy Taco Meat

Servings: 8

Prep Time: 10 minutes

Cook Time: 10 minutes

Ingredients:

- 2 tablespoons olive oil
- 1 small yellow onion, diced
- ½ tablespoon chili powder
- 2 teaspoons dried oregano
- 1 teaspoon garlic powder
- 2 pounds ground beef (80% lean)

Instructions:

1. Turn the Instant Pot on to the Sauté setting and let it heat up.
2. Add the oil to the pot along with the seasonings.
3. Cook for 5 minutes, stirring often, then stir in the ground beef.
4. Sauté for 3 to 4 minutes then close and lock the lid.
5. Press the Manual button and adjust the timer to 10 minutes.
6. When the timer goes off, let the pressure vent for 10 minutes then do a Quick Release by pressing Cancel and switching the steam valve to "venting".
7. When the pot has depressurized, open the lid.
8. Stir everything together and serve hot.

Nutrition: 345 calories, 23g fat, 31g protein, 1.5g carbs, 0.5g fiber, 1g net carbs

Balsamic Beef Pot Roast

Servings: 8

Prep Time: 5 minutes

Cook Time: 40 minutes

Ingredients:

- 3 pounds boneless beef chuck roast
- 1 tablespoon olive oil
- Salt and pepper
- 1 small yellow onion
- 2 cups water
- ¼ cup balsamic vinegar
- ¼ teaspoon xanthan gum

Instructions:

1. Turn the Instant Pot on to the Sauté setting and let it heat up.
2. Add the oil to the pot and season the beef with salt and pepper.
3. Place the beef in the pot (you may need to cut it into two pieces) and cook for 2 to 3 minutes on each side to brown.
4. Sprinkle in the onions then pour in the water and balsamic vinegar.
5. Close and lock the lid then press the Manual button and adjust the timer to 40 minutes.
6. When the timer goes off, do a Quick Release by pressing Cancel and switching the steam valve to "venting".
7. When the pot has depressurized, open the lid.
8. Remove the beef to a bowl and break it up into pieces while you simmer the cooking liquid on the Sauté setting.
9. Whisk in the xanthan gum and simmer until thickened.
10. Stir the beef back into the sauce and serve hot.

Nutrition: 335 calories, 12.5g fat, 52g protein, 1g carbs, 0.5g fiber, 0.5g net carbs

Pork and Lamb Recipes

Balsamic Pork Tenderloin

Servings: 6

Prep Time: 10 minutes

Cook Time: 35 minutes

Ingredients:

- ¼ cup water
- ¼ cup balsamic vinegar
- 3 tablespoons powdered erythritol
- 1 tablespoon olive oil
- 1 (2-pound) boneless pork tenderloin
- Salt and pepper

Instructions:

1. Turn the Instant Pot on to the Sauté setting and let it heat up.
2. Meanwhile, whisk together the water, balsamic vinegar, and powdered erythritol.
3. Add the oil to the pot and the pork tenderloin – season with salt and pepper.
4. Cook the pork until it is browned on all sides, rotating as needed, about 8 minutes total.
5. Pour in the sauce then close and lock the lid.
6. Press the Meat/Stew button and adjust the timer for 35 minutes.
7. When the timer goes off, let the pressure vent naturally.
8. When the pot has depressurized, open the lid. Slice the pork to serve.

Nutrition: 160 calories, 4g fat, 28g protein, 1.5g carbs, 0g fiber, 1.5g net carbs

Easy Lamb with Gravy

Servings: 5

Prep Time: 10 minutes

Cook Time: 90 minutes

Ingredients:

- 1 tablespoon olive oil
- 2 pounds boneless leg of lamb
- 1 teaspoon dried oregano
- Salt and pepper
- ½ cup white wine
- 1 ½ cups water
- 2 tablespoons coconut flour

Instructions:

1. Turn the Instant Pot on to the Sauté setting and let it heat up.
2. Add the oil to the pot and season the lamb with oregano, salt, and pepper.
3. Place the lamb in the pot and cook for 2 to 3 minutes on each side to brown.
4. Pour in the wine and let it simmer for a few minutes then pour in the water.
5. Add the lamb then close and lock the lid.
6. Press the Manual button and cook on High Pressure for 90 minutes.
7. When the timer goes off, let the pressure vent for 20 minutes then do a Quick Release by pressing Cancel and switching the steam valve to "venting".
8. When the pot has depressurized, open the lid.
9. Remove the lamb to a cutting board and keep warm.
10. Press the Sauté button and whisk the coconut flour into the cooking liquid.
11. Cook for 5 minutes or until thickened the season with salt and pepper.

12. Serve the gravy with the lamb.

Nutrition: 405 calories, 17g fat, 52g protein, 4g carbs, 2g fiber, 2g net carbs

Spicy Pork Carnitas

Servings: 10

Prep Time: 5 minutes

Cook Time: 40 minutes

Ingredients:

- 1 tablespoon chili powder
- 2 teaspoons ground cumin
- ¼ teaspoon cayenne
- 5 pounds boneless pork shoulder, cut into large pieces
- 1 cup water
- ½ cup orange juice
- Salt and pepper

Instructions:

1. Combine the chili powder, cumin, and cayenne in a small bowl then rub the mixture into the pork.
2. Place the pork in the Instant Pot then pour in the water and orange juice.
3. Close and lock the lid then press the Manual button and adjust the timer to 40 minutes.
4. When the timer goes off, let the pressure vent for 15 minutes then do a Quick Release by pressing Cancel and switching the steam valve to "venting".
5. When the pot has depressurized, open the lid.
6. Shred the pork and season with salt and pepper then serve hot.

Nutrition: 330 calories, 8g fat, 59.5g protein, 2g carbs, 0.5g fiber, 1.5g net carbs

Braised Lamb Chops

Servings: 4

Prep Time: 10 minutes

Cook Time: 2 minutes

Ingredients:

- 1 tablespoon olive oil
- 8 bone-in lamb chops (about 2 pounds)
- Salt and pepper
- 1 small yellow onion, diced
- ¼ cup low-carb tomato sauce
- 1 cup beef broth

Instructions:

1. Turn the Instant Pot on to the Sauté setting and let it heat up.
2. Add the oil to the pot and season the lamb with salt and pepper.
3. Add the lamb to the pot and cook for 1 to 2 minutes on each side to brown.
4. Remove the lamb chops and add the onion and tomato sauce to the pot.
5. Cook for 2 minutes then stir in the beef broth.
6. Add the lamb then close and lock the lid.
7. Press the Manual button and adjust the timer for 2 minutes.
8. When the timer goes off, do a Quick Release by pressing Cancel and switching the steam valve to "venting".
9. When the pot has depressurized, open the lid.
10. Spoon the lamb and sauce into a serving bowl and serve hot.

Nutrition: 350 calories, 16g fat, 47.5g protein, 2.5g carbs, 0.5g fiber, 2g net carbs

Ginger Soy-Glazed Pork Tenderloin

Servings: 4

Prep Time: 10 minutes

Cook Time: 5 minutes

Ingredients:

- ½ cup soy sauce
- ¼ cup water
- 2 tablespoons fresh grated ginger
- 1 (1-pound) boneless pork tenderloin
- Salt and pepper
- 1 tablespoon coconut flour

Instructions:

1. Whisk together the soy sauce, water, and ginger in a bowl.
2. Season the pork with salt and pepper then add to the Instant Pot.
3. Close and lock the lid then press the Manual button and adjust the timer to 5 minutes.
4. When the timer goes off, let the pressure vent for 10 minutes then do a Quick Release by pressing Cancel and switching the steam valve to "venting".
5. When the pot has depressurized, open the lid.
6. Remove the pork to a cutting board and cover with foil.
7. Stir the coconut flour into the cooking liquid then press the Sauté button.
8. Cook until thickened then slice the pork and pour the glaze over it to serve.

Nutrition: 160 calories, 4g fat, 24g protein, 7.5g carbs, 2g fiber, 5.5g net carbs

Herb-Roasted Lamb Shoulder

Servings: 6

Prep Time: 10 minutes

Cook Time: 40 minutes

Ingredients:

- 1 tablespoon fresh chopped thyme
- 1 ½ teaspoons fresh chopped rosemary
- 1 teaspoon fresh chopped oregano
- 2 ½ pounds boneless lamb shoulder
- Salt and pepper
- 1 cup water

Instructions:

1. Combine the herbs in a small bowl then rub it into the lamb and season with salt and pepper.
2. Place the lamb in the Instant Pot and add the water.
3. Close and lock the lid then press the Manual button and set the timer for 40 minutes.
4. When the timer goes off, let the pressure vent for 10 minutes then do a Quick Release by pressing Cancel and switching the steam valve to "venting".
5. When the pot has depressurized, open the lid.
6. Transfer the lamb to a roasting pan and broil for 10 minutes until browned.
7. Let the lamb rest on a cutting board for 10 minutes before slicing to serve.

Nutrition: 360 calories, 20g fat, 42g protein, 1.5g carbs, 0.5g fiber, 1g net carbs

Curried Pork Shoulder

Servings: 8

Prep Time: 10 minutes

Cook Time: 55 minutes

Ingredients:

- 2 tablespoons olive oil
- 4 pounds boneless pork shoulder, cut into large pieces
- Salt and pepper
- 1 small yellow onion, chopped
- 1 tablespoon fresh grated ginger
- 3 ½ cups unsweetened coconut milk
- 1 tablespoon curry powder

Instructions:

1. Turn the Instant Pot on to the Sauté setting and let it heat up.
2. Add the olive oil to the pot and season the pork with salt and pepper.
3. Add the pork to the pot and cook until browned on all sides, about 8 minutes total.
4. Remove the pork to a cutting board then add the onions and ginger to the pot.
5. Cook for 3 minutes then add the coconut milk.
6. Add the pork back to the pot and sprinkle with curry powder.
7. Close and lock the lid then press the Manual button and cook on High Pressure for 55 minutes.
8. When the timer goes off, do a Quick Release by pressing Cancel and switching the steam valve to "venting".
9. When the pot has depressurized, open the lid.
10. Cut the pork into chunks and stir back into the sauce to serve.

Nutrition: 380 calories, 13.5g fat, 59.5g protein, 2.5g carbs, 1g fiber, 1.5g net carbs

Curried Lamb Stew

Servings: 4

Prep Time: 15 minutes

Cook Time: 50 minutes

Ingredients:

- 1 tablespoon olive oil
- 1 small yellow onion, chopped
- 1 ½ pounds boneless lamb shoulder, chopped
- 2 cups chopped cauliflower
- Salt and pepper
- 1 ½ cups chicken broth
- 1 tablespoon curry powder

Instructions:

1. Turn the Instant Pot on to the Sauté setting and let it heat up.
2. Add the oil then stir in the onions and cook for 4 minutes.
3. Stir in the chopped lamb, cauliflower, chicken broth, and curry powder. Season with salt and pepper.
4. Close and lock the lid then press the Manual button and adjust the timer to 50 minutes.
5. When the timer goes off, let the pressure vent naturally.
6. When the pot has depressurized, open the lid.
7. Stir well and adjust seasonings to taste before serving.

Nutrition: 385 calories, 17g fat, 51g protein, 5.5g carbs, 2g fiber, 3.5g net carbs

Smothered Pork Chops

Servings: 4

Prep Time: 10 minutes

Cook Time: 30 minutes

Ingredients:

- 2 tablespoons olive oil
- 4 (5-ounce) boneless pork loin chops
- Salt and pepper
- 8 ounces sliced mushrooms
- ½ cup heavy cream
- 1 tablespoon butter
- ½ teaspoon xanthan gum

Instructions:

1. Turn the Instant Pot on to the Sauté setting and let it heat up.
2. Add the oil to the pot and season the pork chops with salt and pepper.
3. Place the pork chops in the pot and brown for 3 minutes on each side then remove to a plate.
4. Add the mushrooms to the pot and place the pork chops on top.
5. Close and lock the lid then press the Manual button and cook on High Pressure for 25 minutes.
6. When the timer goes off, let the pressure vent for 10 minutes then do a Quick Release by pressing Cancel and switching the steam valve to "venting".
7. When the pot has depressurized, open the lid.
8. Remove the pork chops to a plate then add the heavy cream and butter to the pot.
9. Sprinkle with xanthan gum then simmer on the Sauté setting for 5 minutes until thickened.
10. Stir the gravy then spoon over the pork chops to serve.

Nutrition: 350 calories, 20.5g fat, 39g protein, 2.5g carbs, 0.5g fiber, 2g net carbs

Rosemary Garlic Leg of Lamb

Servings: 8 to 10

Prep Time: 15 minutes

Cook Time: 30 minutes

Ingredients:

- 2 tablespoons olive oil
- 4 pounds boneless leg of lamb
- Salt and pepper
- 2 tablespoons chopped rosemary
- 1 tablespoon garlic
- 2 cups water

Instructions:

1. Turn the Instant Pot on to the Sauté setting and let it heat up.
2. Add the oil then season the lamb with salt and pepper.
3. Place the lamb in the pot and cook for 2 to 3 minutes on each side to brown.
4. Remove the lamb and rub the garlic and rosemary into it.
5. Place the steamer insert in your pot and add the water.
6. Add the lamb to the steamer insert then close and lock the lid.
7. Press the Meat/Stew button and adjust the timer to 30 minutes.
8. When the timer goes off, let the pressure vent naturally.
9. When the pot has depressurized, open the lid.
10. Let the lamb rest on a cutting board for 10 minutes before slicing.

Nutrition: 365 calories, 16g fat, 51g protein, 1g carbs, 0.5g fiber, 0.5g net carbs

Side Dish Recipes

Spaghetti Squash

Servings: 6

Prep Time: 5 minutes

Cook Time: 5 minutes

Ingredients:

- 1 (4-pound) spaghetti squash
- 1 cup water
- 1 to 2 tablespoons butter
- Salt and pepper

Instructions:

1. Cut the spaghetti squash in half and remove the seeds.
2. Place the squash in the Instant Pot and add the water.
3. Close and lock the lid then press the Manual button and adjust the timer to 5 minutes.
4. When the timer goes off, do a Quick Release by pressing Cancel and switching the steam valve to "venting".
5. When the pot has depressurized, open the lid.
6. Remove the squash and scrape the flesh into a bowl with two forks.
7. Stir in the butter and season with salt and pepper to serve.

Nutrition: 70 calories, 4g fat, 1g protein, 8g carbs, 1.5g fiber, 6.5g net carbs

Lemon Parmesan Zucchini "Noodles"

Servings: 4

Prep Time: 5 minutes

Cook Time: 3 minutes

Ingredients:

- 1 tablespoon olive oil
- 3 cloves minced garlic
- 1 tablespoon fresh lemon zest
- 3 large zucchini, spiralized into noodles
- 2 tablespoons fresh lemon juice
- ½ cup grated parmesan cheese

Instructions:

1. Turn the Instant Pot on to the Sauté setting and let it heat up.
2. Add the olive oil then stir in the garlic and lemon zest.
3. Cook for 60 seconds then stir in the zucchini noodles and lemon juice.
4. Cook for 2 minutes until the noodles are just tender.
5. Stir in the parmesan cheese and serve hot.

Nutrition: 125 calories, 7g fat, 7g protein, 9.5g carbs, 3g fiber, 6.5g net carbs

Garlic Asparagus

Servings: 4

Prep Time: 5 minutes

Cook Time: 2 minutes

Ingredients:

- 1 pound asparagus
- 1 cup water
- 1 tablespoon butter
- 2 cloves minced garlic

Instructions:

1. Place a steamer insert in the Instant Pot and add the water.
2. Add the asparagus to the steamer insert then close and lock the lid.
3. Press the Steam button and set the timer to 2 minutes.
4. When the timer goes off, do a Quick Release by pressing Cancel and switching the steam valve to "venting".
5. When the pot has depressurized, open the lid.
6. Remove the steamer insert and set the asparagus aside.
7. Press the Sauté button and add the butter and garlic.
8. Cook for 1 to 2 minutes then toss in the asparagus.
9. Season with salt and pepper to serve.

Nutrition: 50 calories, 3g fat, 2.5g protein, 5g carbs, 2.5g fiber, 2.5g net carbs

Creamy Mashed Cauliflower

Servings: 4

Prep Time: 5 minutes

Cook Time: 3 minutes

Ingredients:

- 1 cup water
- 2 medium heads cauliflower, chopped
- 2 tablespoons butter
- Salt and pepper

Instructions:

1. Place the steamer insert in the Instant Pot and add the water.
2. Add the cauliflower to the steamer insert.
3. Close and lock the lid then press Manual and cook on high pressure for 3 minutes.
4. When the timer goes off, do a Quick Release by pressing Cancel and switching the steam valve to "venting".
5. When the pot has depressurized, open the lid.
6. Transfer the cauliflower to a food processor and add the butter, salt, and pepper.
7. Blend until the cauliflower is smooth then spoon into a bowl to serve.

Nutrition: 125 calories, 6g fat, 6g protein, 15g carbs, 7g fiber, 8g net carbs

Garlic Green Beans

Servings: 4

Prep Time: 5 minutes

Cook Time: 5 minutes

Ingredients:

- 1 pound green beans, sliced
- 1 cup water
- 2 tablespoons butter
- 3 cloves minced garlic
- Salt and pepper

Instructions:

1. Place the green beans in the Instant Pot.
2. Add the water, butter, and garlic then stir well.
3. Close and lock the lid then press the Manual button and cook on Low Pressure for 5 minutes.
4. When the timer goes off, do a Quick Release by pressing Cancel and switching the steam valve to "venting".
5. When the pot has depressurized, open the lid.
6. Season the beans with salt and pepper and serve hot.

Nutrition: 90 calories, 6g fat, 2g protein, 8.5g carbs, 4g fiber, 4.5g net carbs

Soups and Stews Recipes

Hearty Beef and Bacon Chili

Servings: 4

Prep Time: 10 minutes

Cook Time: 30 minutes

Ingredients:

- 6 slices bacon, chopped
- 2 small red peppers, chopped
- 1 pound ground beef (80% lean)
- 1 cup diced tomatoes
- 1 cup low-carb tomato sauce
- 2 tablespoons chili powder
- 1 teaspoon garlic powder
- Salt and pepper

Instructions:

1. Turn on the Instant Pot to the Sauté setting and add the chopped bacon.
2. Let the bacon cook until it is crisp then remove it with a slotted spoon.
3. Add the red peppers to the pot.
4. Cook for 5 minutes, stirring, then add the rest of the ingredients.
5. Close and lock the lid then press the Bean/Chili button to cook for 30 minutes.
6. When the timer goes off, let the pressure vent for 10 minutes then press Cancel to do a Quick Release by switching the steam valve to "venting".
7. Open the lid when the pot has depressurized and stir in the bacon.
8. Season with salt and pepper to taste then serve hot.

Nutrition: 470 calories, 30g fat, 38g protein, 12g carbs, 3.5g fiber, 8.5g net carbs

Clam and Cauliflower Chowder

Servings: 6

Prep Time: 10 minutes

Cook Time: 10 minutes

Ingredients:

- 3 (6.5-ounce) cans chopped clams
- 3 tablespoons butter
- 1 small yellow onion
- 4 cups chopped cauliflower
- 1 ½ cups heavy cream
- ½ teaspoon dried thyme
- Salt and pepper

Instructions:

1. Drain the clams into a bowl and add water to the juice to make 2 cups of liquid.
2. Turn the Instant Pot on to the Sauté setting then add the butter and onion.
3. Cook for 2 minutes then add the cauliflower and clam juice.
4. Close and lock the lid then push the Manual button and set the timer for 5 minutes.
5. When the timer goes off, let the pressure vent for 3 minutes then press Cancel and do a Quick Release by switching the steam valve to "venting".
6. When the pot has depressurized, stir in the clams and heavy cream.
7. Cook on the Sauté setting until heated through then season with thyme, salt, and pepper. Serve hot.

Nutrition: 250 calories, 17g fat, 17g protein, 9g carbs, 2g fiber, 7g net carbs

Buffalo Chicken Soup

Servings: 6

Prep Time: 10 minutes

Cook Time: 5 minutes

Ingredients:

- 1 tablespoon olive oil
- ½ cup diced yellow onion
- 1 pound boneless chicken thighs, chopped (cooked)
- 4 cups chicken broth
- 3 tablespoons hot sauce
- 6 ounces cream cheese, chopped
- ½ cup heavy cream

Instructions:

1. Turn the Instant Pot on to the Sauté setting and let it heat up.
2. Add the oil then stir in the onion and cook for 3 to 4 minutes.
3. Stir in the chicken, chicken broth, and hot sauce.
4. Close and lock the lid then press the Soup button and adjust the timer to 5 minutes.
5. When the timer goes off, let the pressure vent for 5 minutes then do a Quick Release by pressing the Cancel button and switching the steam valve to "venting".
6. When the pot has depressurized, open the lid.
7. Spoon a cup of the soup into a blender and add the cream cheese.
8. Blend smooth then stir the mixture back into the pot with the heavy cream.
9. Stir until smooth then serve hot.

Nutrition: 345 calories, 28g fat, 19g protein, 2.5g carbs, 0g fiber, 2.5g net carbs

Cheesy Cauliflower Soup

Servings: 4

Prep Time: 5 minutes

Cook Time: 5 minutes

Ingredients:

- 2 tablespoons butter
- 8 cups chopped cauliflower
- 3 cups chicken broth
- ½ cup heavy cream
- 4 ounces cream cheese, chopped
- 1 cup shredded cheddar cheese

Instructions:

1. Turn the Instant Pot on to the Sauté setting and let it heat up.
2. Add the butter and cook for 30 seconds until melted.
3. Add the cauliflower and chicken broth, stirring to coat with butter.
4. Close and lock the lid then press the Manual button and set the timer for 5 minutes on High Pressure.
5. When the timer goes off, press Cancel to do a Quick Release by switching the steam valve to "venting".
6. When the pot has depressurized, open the lid.
7. Puree the soup with an immersion blender then add the heavy cream, cream cheese, and cheddar cheese and stir until the cheese melts.
8. Adjust the seasoning to taste and serve hot.

Nutrition: 395 calories, 32g fat, 17g protein, 13g carbs, 5g fiber, 8g net carbs

Easy Taco Chicken Soup

Servings: 4

Prep Time: 5 minutes

Cook Time: 18 minutes

Ingredients:

- 1 pound boneless chicken thighs, chopped
- ½ cup diced yellow onion
- 2 cups chicken broth
- 1 tablespoon chipotle chilis in adobo, chopped
- 1 tablespoon ground cumin
- 1 (8-ounce) package cream cheese, chopped
- Salt and pepper

Instructions:

1. Turn the Instant Pot on to the Sauté setting and let it heat up.
2. Add the chicken and sauté for 3 minutes, stirring, until browned.
3. Stir in the rest of the ingredients aside from the cream cheese.
4. Close and lock the lid then press the Manual button and adjust the timer to 18 minutes on High Pressure.
5. When the timer goes off, let the pressure vent for 10 minutes then press Cancel to do a Quick Release by switching the steam valve to "venting".
6. When the pot has depressurized, open the lid.
7. Stir in the cream cheese until it is melted and fully incorporated.
8. Season with salt and pepper then serve with fresh cilantro, if desired.

Nutrition: 470 calories, 38g fat, 27g protein, 4.5g carbs, 1g fiber, 3.5g net carbs

Dessert Recipes

Coconut Flan

Servings: 6

Prep Time: 20 minutes

Cook Time: 9 minutes

Ingredients:

- ¾ cup powdered erythritol, divided
- 2 tablespoons water
- 1 cup unsweetened coconut milk
- 1 cup heavy cream
- 2 teaspoons vanilla extract
- Pinch salt
- 3 large eggs

Instructions:

1. Whisk together ½ cup of the powdered erythritol and water in a saucepan over medium heat until it starts to darken.
2. Divide the mixture among six small ramekins and set aside to cool.
3. Combine the coconut milk and cream in a saucepan and cook over medium heat until it starts to steam then whisk in the rest of the erythritol and the vanilla extract.
4. Beat the eggs in a mixing bowl then pour a few tablespoons of the warmed milk into it while whisking.
5. Pour the egg mixture into the milk mixture and whisk smooth then pour into the ramekins.
6. Cover the ramekins with foil and place them in the steamer insert in your Instant Pot.

7. Pour in ½ cup water then close and lock the lid.
8. Press the Manual button and adjust the timer for 9 minutes.
9. When the timer goes off, let the pressure vent naturally then press Cancel.
10. When the pot has depressurized, open the lid.
11. Remove the ramekins and let the flan cool to room temperature then chill until ready to serve.

Nutrition: 205 calories, 19.5g fat, 4.5g protein, 3g carbs, 1g fiber, 2g net carbs

Blueberry Mug Cake

Servings: 4

Prep Time: 5 minutes

Cook Time: 10 minutes

Ingredients:

- 1 1/3 cup almond flour
- 4 large eggs
- ¼ cup sugar-free maple syrup
- 2 teaspoons vanilla extract
- ¼ teaspoon salt
- ½ cup fresh blueberries

Instructions:

1. Place the trivet in the Instant Pot and add 1 cup of water.
2. Whisk together the almond flour, egg, sugar-free maple syrup, vanilla, and salt in a mixing bowl.
3. Fold in the blueberries then divide the mixture among four 8-ounce jars.
4. Cover the jars with foil then place on the trivet, close and lock the lid.
5. Press the Manual button and adjust the timer to 10 minutes.
6. When the timer goes off, do a Quick Release by pressing Cancel and switching the steam valve to "venting".
7. When the pot has depressurized, open the lid.
8. Remove the jars and let them cool a little before serving.

Nutrition: 285 calories, 23g fat, 14g protein, 9.5g carbs, 4g fiber, 5.5g net carbs

Ricotta Lemon Cheesecake

Servings: 6

Prep Time: 10 minutes

Cook Time: 30 minutes

Ingredients:

- 1 (8-ounce) package cream cheese, softened
- ¼ cup powdered erythritol
- 1/3 cup whole-milk ricotta cheese
- Juice and zest of 1 lemon
- ½ teaspoon lemon extract
- 2 large eggs

Instructions:

1. Combine all of the ingredients except the eggs in a mixing bowl.
2. Beat until the mixture is smooth then adjust sweetener to taste.
3. Lower the mixer speed and blend in the eggs until they are fully incorporated, being careful not to overmix.
4. Grease a 6-inch springform pan and pour in the cheesecake mixture.
5. Cover the pan with foil and place it in the Instant Pot on top of the trivet.
6. Pour in 2 cups of water then close and lock the lid.
7. Press the Manual button and adjust the timer for 30 minutes on High Pressure.
8. When the timer goes off, let the pressure vent naturally.
9. When the pot has depressurized, open the lid.
10. Let the cheesecake cool a little then chill for at least 8 hours before serving.

Nutrition: 180 calories, 16g fat, 6.5g protein, 2g carbs, 0g fiber, 2g net carbs

Creamy Lemon Curd

Servings: 6

Prep Time: 10 minutes

Cook Time: 10 minutes

Ingredients:

- 3 ounces butter
- 1 cup powdered erythritol
- 2 large eggs
- 2 large egg yolks
- 2/3 cup lemon juice

Instructions:

1. Combine the butter and erythritol in a mixing bowl and beat for 2 minutes.
2. Whisk together the eggs and yolks then drizzle them into the bowl while mixing.
3. Add the lemon juice and mix until well combined.
4. Divide the mixture among three half-pint jars and loosely cover with the lids.
5. Place the jars in the Instant Pot on the trivet then pour in 1 ½ cups water.
6. Close and lock the lid.
7. Press the Manual button and adjust the timer to 10 minutes on High Pressure.
8. When the timer goes off, let the pressure vent for 10 minutes then do a Quick Release by pressing Cancel and switching the steam valve to "venting".
9. When the pot has depressurized, open the lid.
10. Let the curd thicken for 20 minutes at room temperature then chill.

Nutrition: 150 calories, 15g fat, 3g protein, 1g carbs, 0g fiber, 1g net carbs

Chocolate Pudding Cake

Servings: 8

Prep Time: 10 minutes

Cook Time: 4 minutes

Ingredients:

- 2/3 cup stevia-sweetened dark chocolate
- ½ cup unsweetened applesauce
- 2 large eggs
- 1 teaspoon vanilla extract
- ½ cup almond flour
- ¼ cup unsweetened cocoa powder

Instructions:

1. Melt the chocolate in a double boiler over low heat until melted.
2. In a mixing bowl, whisk together the applesauce, eggs, and vanilla extract.
3. Whisk in the almond flour and cocoa powder then stir in the melted chocolate.
4. Pour the mixture into a greased 6-inch cake pan.
5. Place the pan in the Instant Pot on top of the trivet and pour in 2 cups of water.
6. Close and lock the lid.
7. Press the Manual button and adjust the timer on High Pressure for 4 minutes.
8. When the timer goes off, do a Quick Release by pressing Cancel and switching the steam valve to "venting".
9. When the pot has depressurized, open the lid.
10. Remove the pan and let the cake cool 10 minutes before removing.

Nutrition: 150 calories, 11g fat, 5g protein, 16.5g carbs, 5g fiber, 11.5g net carbs

Mini Vanilla Custards

Servings: 4

Prep Time: 20 minutes

Cook Time: 9 minutes

Ingredients:

- ¾ cup powdered erythritol, divided
- 2 tablespoons water
- 1 cup unsweetened almond milk
- 1 cup heavy cream
- 1 tablespoon vanilla extract
- Pinch salt
- 3 large eggs

Instructions:

1. Whisk together ½ cup of the powdered erythritol and water in a saucepan over medium heat until the erythritol melts.
2. Divide the mixture among four small ramekins and set aside to cool.
3. Combine the almond milk and cream in a saucepan and cook over medium heat until it starts to steam then whisk in the rest of the erythritol and the vanilla extract.
4. Beat the eggs in a mixing bowl.
5. Whisk a few tablespoons of the milk mixture into the eggs then whisk in the rest in a steady stream.
6. Cover the ramekins with foil and place them in the steamer insert in your Instant Pot.
7. Pour in ½ cup water then close and lock the lid.
8. Press the Manual button and adjust the timer for 9 minutes.
9. When the timer goes off, let the pressure vent naturally then press Cancel.
10. When the pot has depressurized, open the lid.

11. Remove the ramekins and let the custards cool for 10 minutes then serve warm.

Nutrition: 175 calories, 16g fat, 5.5g protein, 2g carbs, 0.5g fiber, 1.5g net carbs

Coconut Almond Cake

Servings: 8

Prep Time: 5 minutes

Cook Time: 40 minutes

Ingredients:

- 1 cup almond flour
- ½ cup unsweetened shredded coconut
- 6 tablespoons powdered erythritol
- 1 teaspoon baking powder
- 2 large eggs
- ½ cup heavy cream
- ¼ cup butter, melted

Instructions:

1. Whisk together the almond flour, coconut, erythritol, and baking powder in a mixing bowl.
2. Add the eggs, heavy cream, and butter then whisk smooth.
3. Pour into a greased 6-inch cake pan and cover with foil.
4. Place the steamer rack in the Instant Pot and add 2 cups of water.
5. Put the cake pan on the steamer rack then close and lock the lid.
6. Press the Manual button and adjust the timer to 40 minutes at High Pressure.
7. When the timer goes off, let the pressure vent for 10 minutes then do a Quick Release by pressing Cancel and switching the steam valve to "venting".
8. When the pot has depressurized, open the lid.
9. Remove the cake and let it cool in the pan for 15 minutes before turning out.

Nutrition: 290 calories, 27.5g fat, 5.5g protein, 7g carbs, 3.5g fiber, 3.5g net carbs

Maple Almond Cake in a Jar

Servings: 3

Prep Time: 5 minutes

Cook Time: 10 minutes

Ingredients:

- 1 cup almond flour
- 3 large eggs
- 3 tablespoons sugar-free maple syrup
- 1 ½ teaspoons vanilla extract
- ¼ teaspoon salt

Instructions:

1. Place the trivet in the Instant Pot and add 1 cup of water.
2. Whisk together the almond flour, egg, sugar-free maple syrup, vanilla, and salt in a mixing bowl.
3. Divide the mixture among three 8-ounce jars.
4. Cover the jars with foil then place on the trivet, close and lock the lid.
5. Press the Manual button and adjust the timer to 10 minutes.
6. When the timer goes off, do a Quick Release by pressing Cancel and switching the steam valve to "venting".
7. When the pot has depressurized, open the lid.
8. Remove the jars and let them cool a little before serving.

Nutrition: 275 calories, 22.5g fat, 13.5g protein, 7g carbs, 3.5g fiber, 3.5g net carbs

Easy Chocolate Cheesecake

Servings: 6

Prep Time: 10 minutes

Cook Time: 30 minutes

Ingredients:

- 1 (8-ounce) package cream cheese, softened
- ¼ cup unsweetened cocoa powder
- ¼ cup powdered erythritol
- 1/3 cup whole-milk ricotta cheese
- 1 teaspoon vanilla extract
- 2 large eggs

Instructions:

1. Combine all of the ingredients except the eggs in a mixing bowl.
2. Beat until the mixture is smooth then adjust sweetener to taste.
3. Lower the mixer speed and blend in the eggs until they are fully incorporated, being careful not to overmix.
4. Grease a 6-inch springform pan and pour in the cheesecake mixture.
5. Cover the pan with foil and place it in the Instant Pot on top of the trivet.
6. Pour in 2 cups of water then close and lock the lid.
7. Press the Manual button and adjust the timer for 30 minutes on High Pressure.
8. When the timer goes off, let the pressure vent naturally.
9. When the pot has depressurized, open the lid.
10. Let the cheesecake cool a little then chill for at least 6 hours before serving.

Nutrition: 180 calories, 16g fat, 6.5g protein, 3.5g carbs. 1g fiber, 2.5g net carbs

Classic Crème Brulee

Servings: 6

Prep Time: 5 minutes

Cook Time: 9 minutes

Ingredients:

- 2 cups heavy cream
- 6 large egg yolks
- 3 tablespoons powdered erythritol
- 1 tablespoon vanilla extract
- 2 tablespoons granular erythritol

Instructions:

1. Whisk together the heavy cream, egg yolks, powdered erythritol, and the vanilla in a bowl.
2. Divide the mixture among 6 small ramekins and cover with foil.
3. Place the steamer rack in the Instant Pot and add 1 cup water.
4. Place the ramekins in the steamer rack, offsetting the stacks so they are stable.
5. Close and lock the lid then press the Manual button and adjust the timer to 9 minutes.
6. When the timer goes off, let the pressure vent for 15 minutes then do a Quick Release by pressing Cancel and switching the steam valve to "venting".
7. When the pot has depressurized, open the lid.
8. Remove the ramekins and chill until they are cold.
9. Sprinkle the granular erythritol over the crème brulees and place under the broiler until browned.
10. Let the topping harden before serving.

Nutrition: 200 calories, 19g fat, 3.5g protein, 2g carbs, 0g fiber, 2g net carbs

40026960R00051

Made in the USA
Middletown, DE
22 March 2019